/ maiden voyage /

/ maiden voyage /

poetry

written by

Amber Awni

Written and Edited by Amber Awni

Published by Rainbow Raven Publishing LLC

Paperback ISBN 979-8-9903066-0-8

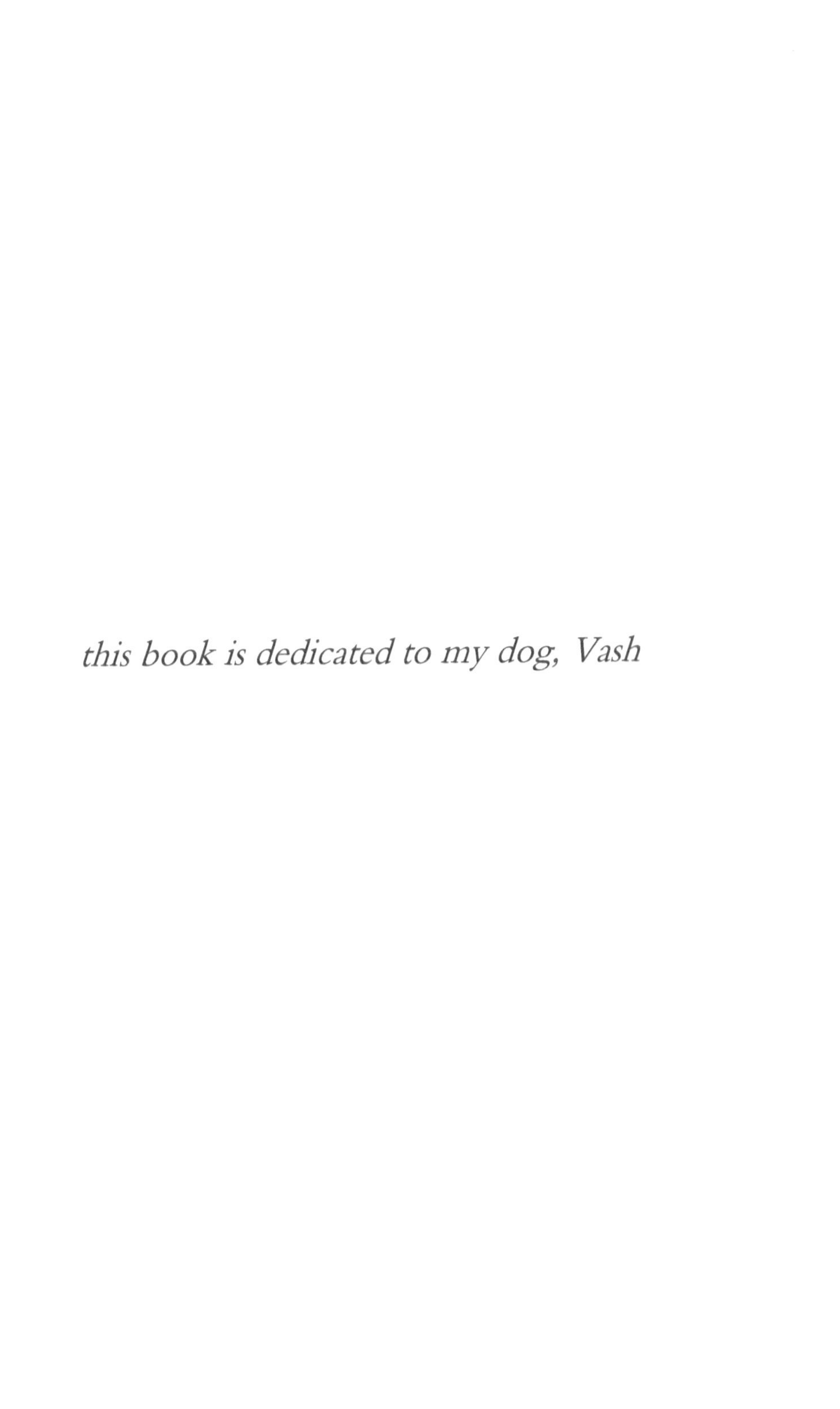

this book is dedicated to my dog, Vash

author's note

hello & thank you so very much for buying this book.

before we continue this journey together, i wanted to say a few words:

art is, and has always been, a rebellious voice against the status quo.

this world is slowly but surely losing art in all forms—movies remade over and over again, architecture around us becoming bleak, color bleached from anything except for advertisements—

artists,

writers,

painters,

illustrators,

sculptors,

all creatives alike,

are not making enough money to justify creating—so they stop completely.

i want you to think for a moment, what do you do when you come home from work every day?

turn on a show, read a book, listen to music, play a video game, bust out a canvas?

humans turn to art, in some form or another, whenever we possibly can.

in art, we find solace, identity, comfort.

in art, we find ourselves.

please, be an ally to artists—authors included.

if, for whatever reason, you do not enjoy this book (or any book, for that matter),

please donate it to your local library instead of returning it.

(you can always 'tear me a new one' in your review)

i am (like you) a human being living under capitalism, and writing books is my livelihood.

(however, i am hoping you will love this collection of poems and decide to write a raving review instead)

★★★

thank you, dear reader.

★★★

table of contents

author's note

table of contents

{foreward}

[dead on arrival]

lost at sea

our relationship: the prologue

susceptible

my birthday party: October 2011

[quickly sinking]

[mold me]//[conform me]

pigtails

our relationship: the highlights

{vault}

easily spotted

{breathless}

puppeteer

{backhanded compliments}

{vault ii}

it started small

things that made me fall in love with you

[incinerate]

{vault iii}

like monarch butterflies

d i s s e c t i o n

mirror on the wall

BAMBER | BAMER | BAMBER |

dogs are a girl's best friend

{vault iiii}

in the alternate reality where i have a brother

[the moment]

{he loves me not}

TIME IS HAPPENING ALL AT ONCE

pirates

[coping or self-destructing]

five finger discount

you wouldn't let me love you

{memories} that i wish would fade

maiden voyage

[if you let me]

the truth is

{epilogue}

acknowledgements

about the author

about the dog

{foreward}

first   a bottle

        sacrifice

        human blood

                a favored god

                lay their hands

                the captain

        a bottle

        the ritual of breaking

                    onlookers gave her

                    a baptism of bourbon

[dead on arrival]

Erasure of My Chemical Romance

sister, i
> never had a chance
>> you can't understand
>>> carry on

lost at sea

<pre>
/ the girl /   was taught
                         how to swim young

how to wade   through a liquid-soaked home

/ the girl /   was not
                     gifted with sea legs

/ the girl /   would often
                         fall victim to the swells

                   that swallowed those around her
</pre>

our relationship: the prologue

i touched a star's surface

felt the heat from solar flares

& i was burned in the end

           [you loved the blaze my body became]

gravitational pull so powerful

i became worthy of your attention

           [i've always had stage-fright]

susceptible

"*in love*"   i am   amorphous

"*in love*"   i become   invisible

"*in love*"   i forget   myself

my birthday party: October 2011

[the setting:] my 1-bedroom apartment in the San
Fernando Valley, hosting a Halloween-themed party for
my 19th birthday

[3 hours in:]

i pass by you

you beckon me closer

ask me to sit down on your thighs

marionette doll reaction time

[quickly sinking]

Erasure of Saint Mela

                              might come running when you call

ain't nowhere for me to go but deeper

but i don't always move as fast as you do

[mold me] // [conform me]

Erasure of My Chemical Romance

give me all your

                     heart and make me

what you want

pigtails

i forget that boys are mean to the girls that they have an eye for

pulling on pigtails, pushing them away

the first time we met, you made fun of the music i said i liked—while you were the one listening to it on your phone's speaker in the breakroom

i take things literally so i fully believed you hated me just for existing until i came to that one band practice

i was there with a different band member

but i'm guessing since you and i worked the night shifts you thought it was about time to talk to me like another human

i was so surprised that i don't remember the contents of the conversation

but i do remember that i was wearing plaid pajama pants

and you decided not to take the opportunity to make fun of me for it

our relationship: the highlights

we were the origin of

      "netflix and chill"

countless late-night calls

       drives &

         complaints

           from your

              roommates

your desire   a heavy-weight wrestler

      outclassing

      the light-weight red flags

you were   throwing around

★★★

blurred nights   turned to

blurred weeks   turned to

blurred months   turned to

   blurred

     years

turned to   your tongue-whipped remarks
turned to   regurgitated demons

★★★

my confidence swallows itself

along with my fingernails

{vault}

the boy turns

      his body into a key

the girl exposes

      her ribcage swinging

open her heart like

      a bank-vault door waiting

the boy swallows

      himself whole

the girl is left

      open & vulnerable

easily spotted

i was never the girl to read romance novels

i imagined worlds where i was loved without words to tell me how

the love-sick twist in my stomach of yearning, knowing it's all just a fantasy

i wore the term "*hopeless romantic*" like it was a badge of honor, unaware i was only slapping a bullseye on my back

in first-person shooters, you always chose the sniper

{breathless}

        one of my fondest memories: your band
was playing a show   post hardcore bodies
        windmilling on the venue's   dance floor
turned mosh pit   the incline in body heat   in
the room   you motioned   me over   as
the singer   hyped up the crowd   i leaned in
you   bent   towards me   embracing the instrument
in your arms   your cheeks   tinged pink   your hair a
dark dagger   growing   from your head
        slicked to a point   with sweat   still
strumming with ease   as you   always do & you
told me   your pedal   board stopped
        working & you knew   i knew your songs
well   enough to manually   change it over for
the electric staff   that you performed   magic with
& i   nodded   cause the speakers   were right
next to us   & you   went back   to your
position   of course   i was wearing a short red
plaid skirt   i'm   sure a lot   of the crowd   saw
my paper-pale   legs turn to pouring   diner coffee
mugs as they dipped   my nervous body   in
sync   with your guitar   strokes &   slight head
nods   it was the moment   early in our   tattoo scab
fresh   relationship   where i realized   you trusted
me   & the way   you looked   when you were
performing   you took   my breath away

& ever since   if i'm not   paying close   enough
attention   i have to remind   myself   how
to breathe   when i'm around you

puppeteer

*the tree on your arm held a skull at its base, like its roots
knew its body was always destined to swallow people
whole. i would trace my fingers along its branches, listen
to you philosophize your past & present fears—how you
seemed to carry your demons in your backpack & your
soul in the strings of your guitar. did i fall in love with
your hands first, or did they always intend to pull me in
with puppeteer strings?*

///

          your
        body   *destined to swallow*

                                                listen
to you philosophize your   *fears*   *you*
        carry your demons in   *your*
soul   *did i fall in*
your hands

///

                               swallow

                                            listen
                             fears
                 demons   *your*
soul   *in*

your hands

{backhanded compliments}

Erasure of The Used

you   always pick the best times
to drop the worst lines
you   made me cry again

{vault ii}

the boy becomes burglar

> *he takes*

the best parts of her

> *inspects them*

in the light

> *throws them*

to the floor

> *he carries*

his baggage in

> *the girl paints*

her outsides

> *with a smile*

a learned habit

it started small

like all things do

small rejections to my softer side

turning away whether it was to my words or touch

threatening not to drive me to work

(when we worked at the same store)

the first time

you pushed me off the bed

when i went to cuddle you good night

i started crying

because i fell

on a corner of plastic

the black milk crates we used as chairs when we had
friends over

a thin red crescent forming on my arm

you told me you hated when girls were emotional

but it wasn't the alcohol

it was what you did

things that made me fall in love with you

when i first met you:

    the way   you   would try to flip   your hair like   it was still long

    the way   you   have this one tooth   in your smile   that reached forward   like a shark's tooth
    it was the only   warning i was given   how your   mouth could tear   a woman to pieces

when you laugh:

    the way   you   cover your face   with one hand   like you were   only half-
way afraid   to show your joy

at night:

    the way   you   let me hold   your heart like it was a burden   for you to wear   & you needed   your chest to breathe

    how you   would share   your mind   with me like   it was a   meal preparing   each thought for   me to digest   until i became
    enthralled with the chef

[incinerate]

Erasure of My Chemical Romance

we are
burning
                        you   incinerate

        every heart you

                hold   on to

        every star fall
brought you to tears

        i've been holding on

can you hear me?

          can
      i s ay

   goodnight
i   n this way
      i stay

{vault iii}

she turns
her cathedral
into a venue
for him
she begs
for him
to fill her
with his music
the boy uses her
for storage
he unpacks
his thoughts
hangs them up
in her head

like monarch butterflies

i

    feel

        endangered

            in

                this

                    climate

d i s s e c t i o n

did you always intend

to pull my wings tight

pin them down on a board

just to stare at the remains

of who i once was

displayed on your wall

★★★

what made you do it

was cracking my skull

open like a walnut shell

worth what you saw inside

my mind a playground

for you to push me around

★★★

the philosopher turned scientist

studying cause & effect

what happens when you fill

a home with flammable fumes

& light a match

mirror on the wall

Erasure of Memphis Mayfire

i don't like who i've become

    i feel like a stranger to myself

                    i wanna hear

     that i'm gonna be fine

i wanna get back

   the broken pieces of

             me   i wanna

    get back to who i used to be

BAMBER | BAMBER | BAMBER |

i'll never understand why you decided to call me this
seemingly innocent nickname why it became your way
to demean me publicly & have it become a silly game for
our friends to join in on i have theorized on it though &
i believe you started calling me this because of the puppy
i adopted from one of our customers how i was potty
training this newborn mammal how i was raising it to be
well-behaved so as not to ever become a problem to you
how i often looked at the small innocent face &
wondered what it would be like to raise children with
you i remember that one argument over my hairbrush
the way you threw it against the wall the way his paws
padded to retrieve the thrown object & when he turned
around the way you softened the way you stopped your
throat's cawing at me to suddenly coo at this creature's
adoration of us the way i envisioned a toddler instead the
way my heart sank like a heavy anchor the dread spread
like a sheet over my corpse the image of our future
children burdened with mom's purple freckles closeted
tears & their silenced voices the foreshadowing of our
future ripped me in two i always thought that my love
for you could drown out your demons but i never
suspected that they would try to take me down with the
ship

dogs are a girl's best friend

they lied to you when they said it was diamonds

diamonds can't save you from abuse

but they sure can trap you in it

they say that diamonds are the strongest known substance
in the universe

but try testing them against a dog's love for his girl

{vault iiii}

   he places a one-way mirror

in front of her

   he drills

his opinions

   into her image

his hateful words

   the girl only sees

herself

   her ears swallow

every word

   & her eardrums smash

each syllable to bite-sized pieces

   they land

on her tongue

   like salt-covered moths

she chokes

   them down

one by one

in the alternate reality where i have a brother

i imagine he is protective of me, his little sister

in this alternative reality, he tells you if you hurt me, he would kill you

he calls me and asks me how you treat me

he comes over and makes sure i know he will always keep me safe from another man's hands

in this alternate reality, my brother finds out the way you talk to me

whether in front of coworkers or friends

or behind closed doors

my brother, in this alternate reality,

comes over to our house with a baseball bat

smashes your amps and guitars and tells you it will be your bones the next time you decide to lay hands on anything other than an instrument or a steering wheel

you and i break up after the first time

because i have a brother

in that alternate world.

[the moment]

[my phone rings.] your twin sister is calling, crying about how her boyfriend, one of your closest friends, is not treating her the way she had romanticized. you, drunk, sitting beside me, snatch the phone away from my hand like popcorn from a bowl, and begin to gnash your teeth in her ear.

[i, the well-trained bitch, leave the room.] but my feet stay planted outside of the shut door, like they have suddenly grown roots into the pine floorboards. i listen to you slur your statements—tell the woman you shared a womb with for over nine months how she has no right to complain because you treat me *so badly* and then

[i am struck by lightning.] the shock ripples through me, electrifying my insides—

—i feel my heart stop, before i take a step away from the confessional booth.

{he loves me not}

i wanted you to love me the way you struggled to dog
paddle through your river of remorse after it was over
between us

i wanted you to love me the way you looked at me when
you had one too many drinks lines and friends over at
our house

the way you seemed so untethered until you saw me

i wanted to be your center of gravity

but i was always just an accessory to you

something glittering to get your hands on

to use and abuse

and you never gave me an answer as to why

you tried to steal my shine

TIME IS HAPPENING ALL AT ONCE

memories like shattered mirror pieces

reflecting images playing out over time

each shard slightly different than the other

the people involved aren't always the same

but the scenes play out like déjà vu

a still-image

a carbon copy

a negative

the never-ending cycle of triggered moments

brain rewired like an old Victorian home

i'm hoping the new contractor in charge

doesn't quit half-way through the job

pirates

you were someone i never suspected

which probably made the heist even easier for you

maybe you decided to take your time with it

maybe you fell for me too

but that didn't change what you stole from me

nor the intent behind the theft

you crept on board

made me believe you were part of my crew

then you began to poison me

first my mind

then my heart

i stopped you before you tainted my soul

[coping or self-destructing]

Erasure of Saint Mela

i guess now i'm avoiding
                                            my   problems

     all these dark spaces   in
    you,
i   sifted through
               when you hit

      m   e   the ceiling
stayed   awake

five finger discount

i think my obsession with hands started

                              when Jack tells Rose
                        that he drew a woman's hands
                        because of their beauty—
i, a nailbiter
from the moment i stepped
into a classroom,
                        could never imagine a life where
                        anyone would find my hands
                        so beautiful,
they would stare at them endlessly,
trying to commit their lines
and curves to memory,
                        using their own fingers
                        and the pages of a book
                        to copy their essence—

i fell in love

with hands, then,

        and their ability to hold,

         their ability to break,

         their ability to heal—

i became obsessed

with the idea of creation—

       have you realized that almost all

        art comes from fingertips?

even Divination has a form

of gazing upon one's hands

to find answers to the future—

         how can we negate

       the power within our palms?

how can i forget

the way

          your hands

         broke me down?

you wouldn't let me love you

i was so gentle

i brushed dust off your cheeks until you snapped at me
that i made you feel like a child

for valentine's day, i decorated our room

everything laced with your favorite color

the color of passion

streamers taped to the ceiling

dollar store doting

that night was the first night i cried myself to sleep next
to you

your back turned to me, that feeling of unwarranted
rejection etched into my soul

all i wanted was to love you, but you wouldn't let me

night after night

year after year

for my birthday, i gifted myself a puppy

and that's when i realized i wasn't impossible to love

you just wanted me to believe i was

{memories} that i wish would fade

{memories} like the mornings i woke up in bliss
{memories} bodies still bare and intertwined {memories}
only to be told the hours held underneath the moon
were erased {memories} i held dear like origami love
letters {memories} you threw away so casually
{memories} like the night of our anniversary
{memories} our roommate's drunk and extremely
attractive friend making a move {memories} me walking
away to cry in our room {memories} you came in locked
the door and showed me you only had eyes for me
{memories} like the last time we made love {memories}
you were sober it was daytime {memories} you told me
you wanted to have the luck of getting me pregnant
{memories} after we finished at the same time
{memories} i started crying {memories} the man i fell in
love with was in front of me {memories} while i had
been loving a cursed version of him for years {memories}
i curse every day for being branded into my skull
{memories} i would kill to be able to erase so easily as
you

maiden voyage

Erasure of Adestria

look to   love to
keep you strong

you've gotta fight
this   hell

face the jaws of death

if

i stand alone
then   i'll scream
until my final breath.

let's

sing. for   this life

if you feel   alone,

                    abandoned and judged, then leave it
all behind and sing

[if you let me]

i would have loved you forever   [if you let me]

i didn't mind when you decided to grow your hair beard
and belly out like a wizard even if you commented on
every inch gained on my belt size

but

i did mind that you lied to me each day

manipulated me at every chance

but

i would have loved you forever   [if you let me]

the truth is

the truth is

      i worked hard for my anger towards you

the truth is

      i used another person   like a cleaver
      made of flesh   to separate us

the truth is

      i knew i would always forgive you

      & you would never change

the truth is

      i didn't want to raise kids with someone
      who would treat me like they hated me

the truth is

      hating you is   the closest
      i'll ever be to   loving you again

Erasure of My Chemical Romance

i keep   the book you gave me

the kiss, the touch
the scar

acknowledgements

thank you, to my dog, for keeping me going when i thought all was lost.

thank you, to my unique and amazing family, for keeping me going, even when i thought i lost myself.

about the author

Amber Awni is a mother of three children, many animals, and sometimes her students. Amber Awni is also an author to several collections of poetry, a small business owner, and a certified silly goose.

Follow Amber Awni by following her publishing company:

https://rainbowraven-publishingllc.mayhem.my/

about the dog

Vash the Stampede was born August 1st, 2013. Amber Awni adopted him in late September 2013. Vash has not only inspired Amber to save herself from an abusive relationship, but also to continue to love herself until all her dreams come true.

Dear Reader,

Thank you so much for reading this collection of poetry.

I am truly grateful that Fate brought my book into your hands.

If you enjoyed this collection, please consider leaving a review on Amazon.

Thank you.